Kickstart Music

3

9-11yrs

MUSIC ACTIVITIES MADE SIMPLE

ANICE PATERSON

DAVID WHEWAY

Contents

First published 2010
by A&C Black Publishers LTD
36 Soho Square, London, W1D 3QY
Copyright © Anice Paterson and David Wheway 2010
ISBN - 978 - 1 - 4081 - 23584
Edited by Laura White
Designed by Sara Oiestad, Jane Tetzlaff & Fi Grant
Cover illustration © David Dean
Inside illustrations © Peter Lubach

A&C Black uses paper produced with elemental chlorine-free pulp, harvested from managed sustainable forests.

Introducing Kickstart

The Kickstart Music series is written specifically with the generalist primary teacher in mind. Kickstart Music 1, 2 and 3 cover the whole of Key Stage 1 and 2, and Kickstart Music Early Years is for under-fives. The authors firmly believe that every teacher can offer a positive musical experience to the children in his or her class.

DEVELOPMENT

The book broadly covers children's development from ages 9–11. However, many of these activities can be used throughout school life, and often simplified for younger or less-experienced children.

STRUCTURE

The materials are divided into five sections. Listening, Rhythm, Movement, Pitch and Sounds and Invention are arranged broadly in progressive order within each section. However, progression in music is not always linear and it is perfectly acceptable for the activities to be used in a different order.
Where it is essential to have completed other activities first, it will say so in the text. All the activities have been tried and tested successfully in the classroom.

Most activities are not just a single lesson plan. Some may last for ten minutes and serve as warm-up activities for others. Some may develop into projects lasting several weeks. Many activities will need re-visiting and further practice to achieve success. Remember that, in music, repeated practice is very important.

The National Curriculum acknowledges that all children within the primary phase of education have an entitlement to musical experiences as an integral part of a broad and balanced curriculum.

The realisation of this entitlement depends on the confidence of the non-specialist teacher in music, as it does in all other areas of the curriculum.

This book has therefore been prepared to support the generalist teacher by:

- Providing a development structure which is achievable.
- Providing outlines of activities which can be extended by teachers as they grow in confidence.
- Making the musical purpose clear and helping the teacher to understand the principles which underpin the musical activity.

Any school using all or most of the ideas will be giving its children a valuable musical experience. In the process, children will be provided with a sound foundation which will meet the requirements of music in the National Curriculum.

Teachers in primary schools should endeavour to:
- Take opportunities to stimulate, sustain and enhance children's interest and awareness of sound.
- Provide a progressive, continuous and relevant musical experience.
- Continually assess and keep a record of each pupil's progress.
- Recognise individual needs and facilitate additional support as and when required.
- Identify what music shares with other areas of the curriculum.
- Develop social skills and awareness through making music together.
- Develop an awareness of, and respect for, musical traditions in a variety of cultures and societies.

Music with your class

Here are some very simple pointers showing how to get the best out of the music activities with your class.

Children copy teachers

If you approach an activity in a positive, energetic and controlled way, the children will do the same.

Keep activities simple

Make sure that you know your materials well.

Children develop at different rates

In music, as in all other areas of the curriculum, keep an open mind about a child's musical potential. Children show it in a variety of ways.

Music is organised sound

It can happen anywhere – in the classroom, the playground, the hall, a music area. It can happen with a variety of sound sources – sounds in the environment, body sounds, sounds and rhythms from 'playing' junk as well as conventional instruments and voices.

Not all activities necessarily lead to a 'performed' product

Try to see performance as part of the process rather than just an end in itself. Encourage children to evaluate their own and other's individual and group performances through careful listening and discussion.

Encourage children to care for instruments

If using instruments with a class, have them ready and close at hand at the start of the lesson to avoid losing time, and don't keep children waiting for too long before using them.

Children bring with them a wealth of musical experience

As well as previous school musical activities, the children may be developing additional skills outside the classroom at home, through instrumental learning or dance classes. Encourage them to be inventive and to value their own ideas and those of other children. Their parents, relations and other members of the local community may also share their musical skills with the class and school.

Develop clear ways of controlling noise

Use definite signals for stopping and starting, and demand immediate response. Give children the opportunity to lead an activity where appropriate. In some music activities, expect lots of noise – try to be tolerant of it. Encourage the tolerance of colleagues by explaining what you are doing and why.

Music helps those with special needs

Music provides opportunities for non-verbal self-expression, communication, motor control, co-ordination and social skills – all areas that are highly valued by the teacher of children with special needs. Many activities promote the opportunity for the development of social skills such as sharing, turn-taking, co-operating with others and appreciating the skills and ideas of other children in their group.

Whole curriculum planning

Activities in this book can support work in other areas of the curriculum. Other obvious inter-relationships may involve skills of a personal or social nature such as co-ordination, discrimination, decision- making, self-confidence, self-discipline, participation, co-operation, tolerance and cultural awareness.

Listening

This section includes activities which develop children's ability to listen carefully with concentration, identify and differentiate between sounds and textures, develop their musical memory and listen and respond to music

Hunt the sound

1. Children in a circle.

2. In pairs around the circle, children choose a voice or body sound. Give them time to try things out before they choose. Make sure it is a sound that both children of the pair can produce.

3. Blindfold two or three children from different pairs (you may like to start with just one child) and mix up the children in the circle.

4. The other children from the pairs make their sound while the blindfolded children find their partners by identifying their sound.

EXTENSION

1. Use a larger space and place children randomly around the room.

2. The children make their sounds more quietly.

3. Rather than sharing the same sound, the partners choose two different sounds and have to remember and locate each others.

4. Children use percussion instruments or other sound makers to make their sound.

5. Use tuned instruments such as chime bars to practise locating their partner by the pitch of the notes played.

PURPOSE
To develop children's ability to identify and locate a specific sound out of many, by its sound quality (or timbre).

RESOURCES

Blindfold or large hat to cover the eyes.

Various instruments for the extension.

Floor turtle

1. Space the children around the hall, all facing the same way. Make up four simple rhythms to go with the following four movements. The rhythms follow the natural rhythm of the spoken sentence, for example:

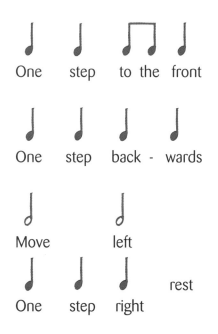

PURPOSE
To enable children to identify and respond to particular rhythms.

RESOURCES

A variety of soundmakers.

A large floor space (eg, hall).

2. Make sure the children can identify by listening which movement goes with which rhythm. Practise until the children know the rhythms and movements well.

3. The children move around the hall following the rhythmic instructions played by the teacher.

EXTENSION

1. Try the same activity with new rhythms and new movements, for example:

Two steps left ♩ ♩ ♩ rest

Wave hands in the air ♩ ♩ ♫ ♩

2. Choose one child at a time to play and choose which movements other children will do.

Writing it down

1. Decide beforehand the different sounds and patterns you are going to make and arrange instruments appropriately. You could play, for example, a cymbal crash, a scraping guiro, a tapping table or a tinkling triangle.

2. Each child has a piece of plain paper and crayons, folds the paper into 4 and numbers each quarter on both sides (8 rectangles).

FRONT

1	3
2	4

BACK

5	7
6	8

3. Play the sounds to the children one at a time. Wait between each one so that the children have the time to draw an image that represents the sound they hear.

4. Share the results. Talk about the similarities, discussing why certain sounds might suggest particular 'pictures'.

EXTENSION

1. Make a series of flash cards using a variety of the children's drawings. Agree how each card should be played. A child points to the cards one by one while the class play them.

2. Children choose their own order of drawings to create their own music piece, first as a class, later in groups. The children might repeat the cards, play them backwards or play more than one at a time.

3. Discuss ways of refining the symbols so that they convey more precise information about dynamics (how loud and soft) and tempo (the speed).

PURPOSE

To encourage children to explore sounds and develop the relationship between visual symbols, shape, colour, line and sound.

RESOURCES

A variety of sound makers.

Paper and coloured crayons.

REMEMBER

Try not to put ideas into their heads – there is no correct answer. Ensure the children do not look at anyone else's drawing. It is very easy to be influenced by others' drawings and not make your own decisions.

Computer recording

The key activities and processes in recording using the computer are:

1. **Recording:** The process of laying down some sound input – voice or instruments.

   Practise with something simple: For example, the children say their names several times in rhythm. Record and play straight back. Save under their names. You can use the clips later.

2. **Editing:** The process of manipulating the recorded material.

   Delete: Scroll to any point in the recording to delete parts of the recording or trim the beginning or end of recordings before saving.

   Alter and adapt: Try recording unusual, imitative or everyday sounds then alter the sounds using the 'Effects' drop down menus. For example, you might want to:
   - Increase or decrease speed.
   - Reverse the sounds – a single ringing triangle or cymbal sound can be very effective. Record someone's name backwards – then reverse it to see if it still sounds like their name.

   Mix: Mix with other files and create simple mixes of sound layers and sound stories.

3. **Appraisal:** Record a verse of a song, a composition or short performance. Ask the children to listen and suggest ways they might improve their vocal or instrumental technique, such as, clarity, playing/singing together, maintaining a steady beat, emphasising certain sounds/words, quality of singing without shouting, playing at the right time.

   Practise and then record again. Play back to note improvements. Save such recordings for the children's assessment records or to place in a listening area. Play again later in the year to note improvements in individual, group or class performance.

PURPOSE
To use the computer to record children's music work in the classroom and improve their work as a result.

RESOURCES

Microphone and speakers .

Audio recording programme eg, 'Audacity'.

Whiteboard speakers will amplify playback more than adequately. Older PCs and laptops pre 'Vista' come with a useful version of 'Sound Recorder' or 'Garage Band' on Apple Macs.

'Audacity' is free to download (search online for 'Audacity').

Children can regularly record their own and others' work in this way once the software has been mastered.

Jingle time

1. Listen to each extract and ask the children to identify or guess the product being advertised.

2. Discuss what musical 'clues' are there to underline the type of product – rhythm, speed, melody, instruments, mood, overall style.

3. Ask the children to invent their own product and devise the words and music to advertise it. Play the results to the class.

EXTENSION

1. Use a DVD video recording with several adverts on it. Turn the volume off when you play them to the class. Children watch it, discuss it, and then invent their own sound track to go with each advert. Play the results along with the recording.

2. Use this activity as part of a cross-curricular project looking at advertising in different ways – for example, artwork, language, drama, citizenship.

PURPOSE
To enable children to explore and analyse the way in which music is used in advertising.

RESOURCES
Recordings, possibly via the Internet, of excerpts from well-known adverts (avoid words which identify the product) using a mixture of styles and products, eg. children's food, cars, chocolate, perfume.

REMEMBER
Children can use any medium to produce this music that they wish. Make sure a range of instruments, sound makers and the computer are available to use if they choose.

This activity may take several sessions to reach performance.

Try 'Opposite Moods' p56, with this activity.

Copycat tunes

1. Two children sit in the middle of a circle facing each other, each with a glockenspiel or xylophone.

2. All the children forming the circle close their eyes.

3. One child in the centre plays a short, simple tune using two or three notes. The second child copies it and plays it back.

4. If it is copied correctly, all the children round the circle put their thumbs up. If it is incorrect they put thumbs down and the child tries again to correct it.

5. Repeat and/or choose two different children to sit in the circle.

6. Later, children work in pairs round the circle – one child singing a tune, the others copying.

EXTENSION

1. Add more notes to the instruments to increase the complexity.

2. One child draws the shape of a tune with their hands; the second child plays the tune back. To do this, children need to be able to remember the tune they have made up and play it again and again the same way. This takes practice and hard, musical concentration.

PURPOSE
To develop children's listening and musical memory.

RESOURCES

Two xylophones or glockenspiels with a limited number of notes on them.

Play it by ear

1. With the whole class, make a short list of simple songs that everyone knows, for example, Christmas carols, nursery rhymes, folk and popular songs.

2. Children work in pairs or small groups with a variety of pitched instruments.

3. Children choose one song to work on and work out how to play it by trial and error. They work on their tune, listening carefully all the time.

4. When it is practised well enough, the children play their tune with the whole class singing along for a verse.

Ideas for songs
Simple tunes for those having difficulty are:

'Frère Jacques'
'Doh, a deer, a female deer'
'Kum ba yah'

In each case, it is safe to start the tunes on a C. Find the notation for these tunes if you wish at the Kickstart Music area of www.acblack.com/music.

PURPOSE
To encourage children to work out how to play music by ear.

RESOURCES
A variety of pitched instruments.

REMEMBER
Do not be tempted to help too much – the children will come to rely on that help. Practice is very important. The children will remember their tune and how to play it more successfully if they work it out for themselves. Children may also choose to play a phrase each in their pairs instead of the whole song.

Sound sequence

1. The children sit or stand in a circle.

2. Each child chooses an individual sound using voice or hands - for example, whistling or tapping hands on thighs.

3. Walk around the circle listening to each sound. If any are too similar and might be confusing, ask one of the children to choose a different sound.

4. Around the circle, the children perform their sound one after another until they become familiar with the order. Each child remembers the sound that precedes their sound in the circle.

5. Everyone spreads out around the room, with no one standing next to the same person as before.

6. Children close their eyes. The class reproduce the sounds in the same order as they were heard in the circle.

Sounds in the circle

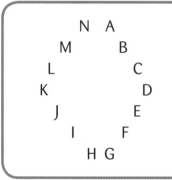

Everyone plays when spread out

```
A       K           C

    G     L     H     M
            B           I


    D           F   J  N
            E
```

PURPOSE
To develop children's concentration and careful listening.

RESOURCES
A large floor space.

A variety of instruments.

REMEMBER

This needs a quiet area to be successful. It requires a lot of concentration.

It is useful to have done 'Hunt the sound' first on p5.

EXTENSION
Repeat the activity above using instruments instead of voices and hands – circle first, spread out second.

Graphics

1. Select a box from the chart below. Who can find a sound for the symbol?

2. The volunteer repeats their sound for the class. Discuss the sound that the child makes for that symbol and ask if someone else can make the same sound.

3. Ask for the sound contained in another box and repeat 2 above.

4. As the children progress add extra instruments until three or more are being passed around the circle.

EXTENSION

1. Arrange the symbols into another order and play again, varying the dynamics, speed, type of instrument or playing more than one at a time.

2. Find images on the web and find sounds or phrases to play that suit them. Construct a chart to play them using the computer. Arrange them in order to make a longer piece.

PURPOSE

To develop children's concentration and careful listening. To increase their awareness of the use of sounds and symbols.

RESOURCES

A large chart as below: Copies for each child or displayed on a white board.

One instrument for each child.

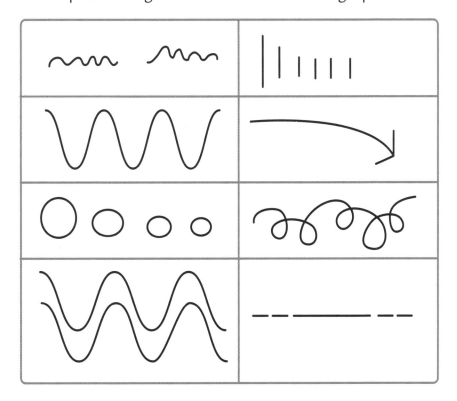

Recording and listening

PURPOSE
To use the recording of children's work as a learning activity.

RESOURCES
Recording device with microphone.

Music the children have written or a song they have performed and recorded.

REMEMBER
The activity will be more worthwhile if the quality of the recording is high.

Recording children's work is rather like putting their paintings on the wall – it shows their work is valued and allows it to be kept and played back. It also helps the children to remember their piece without needing the ability to write or read music.

1. Make a special recording of a piece of children's work or a performance of a song.

2. Talk about the circumstances in which they performed it. Remind them of the original performance requirements and make it feel as if it were a fully professional recording. Put the title and the composers' names up on the wall. Maybe even a photograph or a mock-up of a CD cover!

3. Play the recording to the class and ask questions such as:
   What is the piece about? – Does it have a storyline or is it more abstract? What did the composers intend?
   How good is the recording? – Is it clear or muffled? Were the microphones in the right place? Did we miss things? What could have been done to improve it?
   What do you think of the performers and the performance?
   - What instruments or voices did they use?
   - Could they play them well enough?
   - Did they keep time?
   - Could you hear the words?
   - Did they begin and end exactly together?
   - Was it well in tune?
   - Is the piece too long/short?
   - What else could you improve?

4. Children write up the recording as they would a book review.

REMEMBER

a) The better the recording and playback equipment, the better the result.

b) Do not put a microphone too close to the source of the sound. It will pick up the mechanics – like breathing, a scraping bow or putting down a stick.

c) Where there is a recording volume indication on the machine, do not allow the whole piece to be recorded in the red zone. It will be very distorted. On the other hand, do not record too low or there will be too much hiss on the playback.

d) Generally built-in microphones are not as good or as flexible as separate ones, although portable MP3 recorders are usually small enough to be handheld, solid state (no moving parts) and allow the recorder to get close to the sound source.

EXTENSION

1. **Recording skills.** Spend time showing the class how to set up a recording. Find occasions for some children to record the musical work of others – their musical ideas, someone singing a song, and so on. Those who become sufficiently skilled at it could record the work of other classes from time to time. See the guidance below.

2. **Sing and record.** Divide the children in to groups and ask them to make up a simple song or piece using a variety of instruments. Ask the children to perform while another child records it. Play the recording back and ask the questions (step 3 on page 14) to help the children improve their piece and/or the quality of the recording.

3. **Use computer software to record and manipulate.** There are many programmes which are downloadable from the web for instance 'Audacity' and 'Garage Band'. For more information on music and technology visit the Kickstart Music area of www.acblack.com/music.

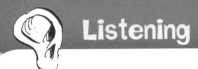

Give it back

All of these exercises and games can be used by the teacher with children, or by children in pairs. All are infinitely adaptable according to the level of ability and musical attainment of the children.

1. The teacher sings a tune – children sing it back.
   The teacher sings a longer tune – children sing it back.

2. The teacher taps a rhythm – children tap it back.
   The teacher taps a longer rhythm – children tap it back.

3. The teacher sings a tune – children tap the rhythm of it back.

4. The teacher writes a rhythm down – children tap it back.

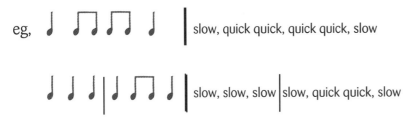

5. Play sequences of notes – play them back.

6. Write sequences of notes down:
   - Play them back.
   - Sing them back.

EXTENSION

1. Children lead. Children make small groups. One child is chosen as the leader. The leader does what the teacher did: Sings a tune or taps a rhythm and the other children sing or tap back.

2. Identify instrumental sounds. Children sit in a circle. Children close their eyes to listen. Choose an instrument and play a rhythm. Ask the children what they heard:
   - Which of these three drums did I play?
   - Which glockenspiel did I play – the large or small one?
   - Which triangle am I hitting – the large or small one?
   - Is this tube I am hitting made of metal, wood or plastic?

PURPOSE
To improve and refine children's listening skills.

RESOURCES
A variety of instruments.

REMEMBER
Don't spend too much time on explanations – just do it – and keep doing it. The children who are left behind at the beginning will catch up if you keep doing it and the others will get plenty of reinforcement.

Make up any tunes or rhythms that come into your head – don't spend time thinking about them. The children will copy whatever you do. There are no right or wrong answers.

Rhythm

This section includes activities which encourage children to develop a strong sense of pulse and rhythmic memory, to hear music in their heads, and to understand the use of repetitions to make music. Many will also help to develop their co-ordination and control of their bodies to help them play instruments.

Drumming

1. Children drum their fingers on a table and play the rhythms below. Keep each set of beats going several times to make a steady rhythm. Fingers in order with the thumb hitting harder than the fingers:
   a) Thumb, 2, 3, 4, 5, thumb, 2, 3, 4, 5.
   b) Alternate the order of the fingers: 1, 3, 2, 4, 3, 5   1, 3, 2, 4, 3, 5.
   c) Play two fingers together: 1 & 3, 2 & 4, 3 & 5.
   d) Play the same three exercises above, but with the opposite hand to the one used before. Make sure both lots of fingers get the same amount of practice to strengthen them equally.
   e) When any exercise has become easy, play it faster until it is hard again.
   f) Make it harder by playing both hands together.

2. Introduce hand drumming on a table. Play:
   L = left hand   R = right hand   :| = repeat

   a) L   R R | L   R R   :|

   b) R R R R | R R R R   :| Both hands
         L   L | L   L   playing together)

   c) R L L L | R L L L   :|

   d) L R R L R R L R | L R R L R R L R :|

PURPOSE

To develop children's co-ordination skills for drumming, keyboard and any other instrument playing.

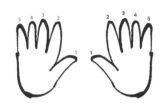

REMEMBER

All of these exercises are easy when done slowly and harder fast. If no one can do it, slow down. If it is too easy, speed it up. This is good for anyone of any age learning or wanting to play an instrument.

This should be repeated on many occasions to improve. Set it for homework.

EXTENSION

Children can make up endless patterns and use them to accompany songs.

Song

1. Decide on a well known song and sing it to the children. They join in when they are ready and confident.

2. Start experimenting with the song in some of the following ways:
   - Say the words together.
   - Clap and say the words together.
   - Clap the rhythm only.
   - Play the rhythm on any instrument.
   - Invent some movements to go with it.

3. Children work in pairs. They choose another song between them and work through the same process. Later they 'test' the whole class to see if they can guess what song it is.

4. Choose one of the songs that worked well in a pair and try it with the whole class.

EXTENSION

1. Children work in small groups. Each group has two or three notes of tuned percussion to use. The children make up new tunes for the song, using the same rhythm but only the notes that they have been given.

2. Share the ideas by asking each group to perform to the class.

PURPOSE
To encourage children to experiment with words and rhythms.

RESOURCES

A well known song.

Instruments. Ideas and notation can be found at the Kickstart Music area of www.acblack. com

REMEMBER

This activity can be spread over several lessons, building an experience and accumulating 'repertoire'.

Sentences

1. Write a selection of short sentences on the board, for example:

- · I like fish and chips.
- · Vinegar and sausages.
- · Bread and jam.

2. Practise as a whole class saying the sentences rhythmically to a pulse. The phrase will find its own rhythm in this way: 'Bread and jam, bread and jam, bread and jam…' Think of it as a musical sentence.

3. Tap the rhythm of the phrase while you continue to chant the words.

4. Ask the children to devise ways of writing the rhythms down without the words, for example, the rhythm of 'I like fish and chips' might be written like one of these:

Discuss which is clearest and easiest to read and write.

5. Ask the children to think up their own phrases that will produce different rhythms.

EXTENSION

1. Can the children fit two sentences together rhythmically at the same time?

2. Play the rhythmic patterns on instruments. Play them in sequence, at the same time, or as a round.

3. Clap a rhythm for the children to write down in their chosen graphics/ notation. Ask them to make up words which fit these rhythms.

4. Use the pentatonic scale (see illustration) to produce a melody using the rhythm patterns, for example:

C	E	G	A	G
I	like	fish	and	chips

PURPOSE
To develop the children's ability to read, play and write rhythm patterns.
To set words to rhythm and melody.

RESOURCES
A writing board that everyone can see.

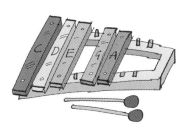

19

Rhythm layers

1. Three children count 1–8 regularly, repetitively and quietly. If need be, the teacher can play a very gentle beat on the drum while the children count.

2. Other children use body sounds, eg. clapping, foot stamping, finger clicking, to play when the three children and/or the teacher say the numbers that are circled on the chart (see below). As they do so at a steady speed beat, a regular rhythm will emerge.

3. Make sure each line is correct rhythmically before proceeding to the next.

4. Next, divide the class into groups. Each group is responsible for one of the lines on the chart. Give each group time to practise their given line.

5. Build up the layers of rhythms. Group 1 play their rhythm and keep it going. Then group 2 join in, then group 3 and so on.

6. Finally, try it with a very quiet drum beat only (without the counting group) so that every child has to count in his head.

EXTENSION

Try this with instruments, pitched and unpitched. Pitched instruments would produce some very interesting harmony. Play it several times to make a more extended piece.

①	2	3	④	5	6	7	8
1	②	3	④	5	6	7	8
①	2	3	④	⑤	6	7	⑧
1	②	3	④	⑤	6	⑦	⑧
①	2	3	4	5	6	7	⑧
①	②	3	4	5	⑥	7	⑧

PURPOSE

To enable children to find some interesting rhythm patterns, both regular and irregular; and to develop their inner pulse.

RESOURCES

A variety of instruments.

A chart (see below).

Echo clapping

1. Tap out a pulse of 4 to the class. The strong beat is bold:

   1 2 3 4 | **1** 2 3 4 | **1** 2 3 4   etc.

2. The children copy it and take over.

3. The children maintain the pattern of 4. Now clap a new repeated pattern over their pattern. It will sound like this:
   eg.

   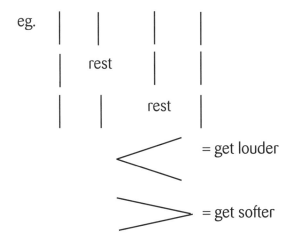

   pulse

   new pattern

4. Children change their pattern to the new one and maintain it. The teacher begins another new repeated pattern over the top. And so on until everyone has grasped the idea.

5. Next include some silent beats and vary the volume:

   eg.

   rest

   rest

   < = get louder

   > = get softer

PURPOSE
To develop children's rhythmic memory and invention.

REMEMBER

To keep strictly in time. This requires a lot of concentration to keep it going accurately.

EXTENSION

1. Try it over a variety of pulses – 3, 5, 7 etc.

2. Small groups of children decide on a leader and play the game together.

Keeping a pulse

1. Ask the children to make a circle around the room. Number the children 1 – 4. Practise saying their numbers round the circle absolutely in time:

    1 2 3 4 │ **1** 2 3 4 │ **1** 2 3 4 etc.

2. Choose one number to be a 'silent' beat:

    1 2   4 │ **1** 2   4 │ **1** 2   4 etc.

3. Choose a different number to be the 'silent' beat and practise saying the numbers again – try nodding in the gap to keep it in time:

    1   3 4 │ **1**   3 4 │ **1**   3 4 etc.

4. When the children are confident and skilled at this, move them into four groups: All the 1's together, all the 2's together and so on.

5. Place the groups around the room.

    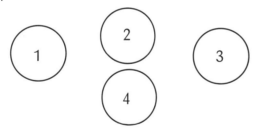

6. Choose a conductor to stand in the middle.
    Keep the beat steady with either a gentle drum or with the recorded music. The four groups say their numbers as before, in order and in time.

EXTENSION

The conductor indicates a silent beat by holding up 1, 2, 3 or 4 fingers. Whenever he changes the number, the silent group start up again and a new group is silenced.

PURPOSE
To develop children's ability to keep a pulse. To improve concentration.

RESOURCES

A drum, a recorded piece of music with a strong, steady beat or a rhythm in 4 time from an electronic keyboard.

Classroom drumming

1. Using any utensil, children first find some interesting sounds in the classroom, eg, scratch a chair, tap the door handle, hit the carpet, twang a wooden ruler.

2. Make a pattern with their sound, for example:

| Scratch tap tap | Hit tap tap | Scratch tap tap |

3. Use any suitable pattern the children have found to accompany a song they know. In this case 'There's a hole in my bucket'.

There's a	hole in my	buc - ket, dear	Li - sa dear	Li-sa
	scratch		scratch	
	tap tap	tap tap	tap tap	
		hit		hit

Try using symbols to represent each song and play:

M		M	
	x x		x x	x x	
	☐			☐

PURPOSE
To develop children's rhythmic co-ordination.

RESOURCES

Rulers, pencils, sticks, beaters, hands.

REMEMBER

Anything can become an instrument if it is used musically, with the sounds arranged in patterns. Once done, all this can be converted onto instruments.

Classroom dancing

Using recorded music (see resources, p64), the teacher leads a rhythmic dance session in one or more of the following ways:

1. Start with a piece with a regular count of four – a rock beat or a march.

   Teacher: 'Give me a **one**, a **two**, a **one**, two, three, four'
   Children: 'a **one**, a **two**, a **one**, two, three, four'

   Do the actions below, the children following the teacher.
   Keep the words and actions completely in time with the music.
   Repeat lots of times.

   March, march, march around the room;
   March, march, march around the room;
   Hop, hop, hop around the room;
   Hop, hop, hop around the room;
   Run, run, run around the room;
   Run, run, run around the room; (double-time steps)
   And flop, flop, flop down on the floor.

   And so on – make up your own movements and words to fit the music (stretch, flop, crouch, jump).

2. Change the music to a fairly slow count of 3, 5 or 6 – or use some Latin American music. Spend time thinking about lazy, smooth movements still ensuring that all are responding to the pulse of the music accurately. Try doing this while sitting in chairs.

   This activity is trying to cement a physical rhythmic response to music so that it becomes second nature to feel the pulse in music.

EXTENSION

Children work in pairs. Put on a new piece in a new style. They identify the pulse and invent movements. While the music is on, call out for all to watch different groups for a few seconds – as if they had the spotlight on their 'routine' for a short time.

PURPOSE
To further develop children's rhythmic co-ordination and response to music.

RESOURCES
Keyboard rhythm box, drum machine software such as '2-beat', 'ESP Rhythm Maker' or freeware such as 'Hammerhead'. Recordings of music with a very strong beat. Use of a large space, such as the hall.

REMEMBER
At this age, aim for the children to be able to keep exactly in time so it becomes a dance. When they stretch, expect them to really extend in a very controlled manner and do all the actions with some real physical precision. Use more sophisticated music than you would with younger children.

Rhythms and tunes

'Through the teeth and past the gums,
Look out stomach, here it comes!'

1. Make sure the whole class knows the rhyme well and, through repetition, can feel its rhythm. It often helps to 'translate' it into rhythm sounds, for example:

   'Through the teeth and past the gums'
   Da   di   da   di   da   di   dum

2. Divide the children into groups and give each a pitched instrument to reproduce the rhythm as a tune. They can sing along when they have worked something out.

3. Listen as a class to all the tunes and discuss them in terms of accuracy of rhythm and interest in the tune.

4. Use non-pitched percussion to play a simple rhythm to accompany the tunes.

5. Practise playing and singing the whole thing faster.

PURPOSE
To encourage children to improvise melodically within a rhythmic framework.

RESOURCES

A variety of instruments, pitched and unpitched.

A poem/limerick the children know well.

REMEMBER

Give children plenty of time to experiment. Tunes are likely to be more successful if the children are limited to just a few notes (see 'Sentences' pentatonic scale, p19).

The repetition of notes is used very commonly and can produce very musical results.

Accompanying songs

PURPOSE
To enable children to find interesting ways to accompany singing with rhythms.

REMEMBER

Listen to the result and alter anything you are not happy with. Notice how the strong beat marked in bold is always after the barline.

1. Choose a song that all of the children know. Make sure they know it very well before beginning.

2. Decide what the pulse of the song is. Are there 3 counts or 4 counts? For example:

1	2	3	**1**	2	3	**1**	2	3
Mor	ning	has	bro	-	-	ken	-	-

1	2	3	**1**	2	3	**1**	2	3
like	the	first	mor	-	-	ning	-	-

or

1	2	3	4	**1**	2	3	4
Carry	mi	ackee	go a	Linstead		Market	

1	2	3	4	**1**	2	3	4
Not a		quatty	wot	sell	-	-	-

3. Tap out the pulse – **1**, 2, 3, or **1**,2,3,4 – making beat 1 the loudest. Keep the tapping going and sing the tune along with it. The pulse is now acting as an accompaniment.

All melody lines for songs mentioned in this book can be found in the Kickstart Music area of www.acblack.com/music.

EXTENSION

1. Use several of the rhythms provided on an electronic keyboard and work out where the strong beat is. Try a waltz for 'Morning has broken' or one of the Latin American ones for 'Linstead Market'. Decide on actions and play along with it. When it's going well, sing your song along with it.

2. Ask a parent or friend of the school who plays the drum kit to bring theirs in to show the children how to play it. Make sure they analyse every action necessary to play it well – and the co-ordination needed to do so. Sing the song you have been working with, with the drum kit as accompaniment.

4. Produce variants of the pulse in different ways. The first beat is usually the strongest:

a) Body sounds:

1	2	3		1	2	3
stamp	click	click		stamp	brush	rest

b) Objects in the classroom:

1	2	3		1	2	3
desk	chair	chair		floor	chair	rest

c) Instruments, eg, drum and bells:

1	2	3		1	2	3
drum	rest	bells		drum	rest	bells

5. Accompany each verse on a different instrument. This can change the mood and sound quality enormously. Try playing on beat 1 only.

6. Give children a choice about which music they would like to hear more of. The Internet now offers opportunities for children to search for extracts (see resources list on p64).

Write it down

1. Children spread out around the hall.

2. Everyone says 'Slow, slow, quick quick, slow' several times to the teacher's hand clap.

3. The children move about the hall in time with the clapping – 'slow, slow, quick, quick, slow' – taking care to take smaller and quicker steps for the 'quick quick'.

4. Add 'long' to the movement, for example: 'Slow, quick quick, slow, quick quick, long, long'. Ask the children to say this along with the clapping.

5. The children move around the hall to this new rhythm, taking twice as long steps for the 'long'.

6. Back in the classroom, try writing the rhythms down. Draw feet instead of notes to begin with:

eg, slow,   slow, quick quick slow

slow slow qu qu slow long long

When the concept is well understood, use the rhythms of names, or poems.

eg. John Wesley

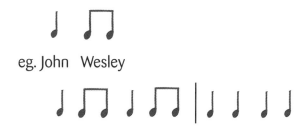

What shall we do with the drunken sailor?

PURPOSE
To improve children's ability to feel rhythms and write them down.

RESOURCES

Paper and pencils.

A very large space such a the school hall.

Movement

This section includes activities which will help children to move freely and rhythmically to music, develop strong co-ordination for the playing of instruments and explore their feeling responses to music.

Hand Singing

1. Sing the song 'My bonnie lies over the ocean'. Teach it to the children over a couple of sessions. When they know it well, try the actions.

2. Use hand signs to 'illustrate' the words of the song. Move hands in the direction of the arrows/lines below. Practise the hand movements carefully.

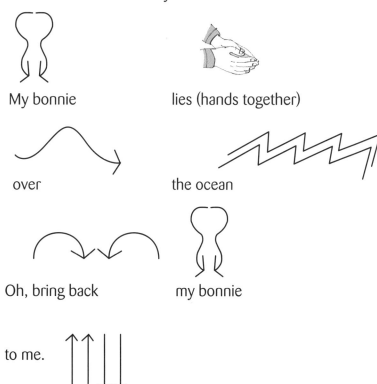

My bonnie

lies (hands together)

over

the ocean

Oh, bring back

my bonnie

to me.

PURPOSE
To improve children's co-ordination while concentrating on another activity.

Ideas for songs
Use other songs and devise actions for them eg, 'Row, row, row your boat'

'She'll be coming round the mountain when she comes'

'The hokey cokey'

Melody lines for these tunes can be found at the Kickstart Music area of www.acblack.com/music.

3. Once the song and the movements are well know, sing the song faster. Then at a faster speed still. Can they still do the movements accurately?

Number patterns

1. Divide the class into two groups. Each child secretly chooses a number between 1 and 3 or 1 and 5.

2. Give one group an instrument each. The rest of the children move into space.

3. Keep a steady pulse by counting out loud:

1 2 3 | **1** 2 3 | **1** 2 3 | **1** 2 3 | **1** 2 3 | **1** 2 3 |

or

1 2 3 4 5 | **1** 2 3 4 5 | **1** 2 3 4 5 | **1** 2 3 4 5

4. Children with instruments make a sound on their chosen number. Children without instruments move on their number. A pattern of sound and movement will emerge.

5. Gradually internalise the pulse. Transfer the beat onto a drum gently. The counting gets softer. Do it silently – the children count in their heads. The drum gets softer and softer until it disappears and everyone is 'feeling' the beat only.

EXTENSION

1. Use a different number of beats, for example, 4, 7 etc.

2. Children pick two or more numbers to move or play on.

3. Agree that some beats are silent, loud or soft.

4. Play with unpitched percussion only – or with pitched percussion only. The musical result will be very different.

PURPOSE
To explore patterns in sound and movement and improve concentration.

RESOURCES
A variety of instruments (chime bars are particularly effective).

REMEMBER

Listen carefully to the resulting 'music'. Sensible suggestions will only follow if the children have really heard and felt the pattern which emerges.

The objective is to feel and hear the patterns in sound and space. However, the next time you do this activity, make sure a different group of children play rather than move. The result feels different depending on which you are doing.

Sequence building

1. Children sit in a circle.

2. One at a time round the circle, children make a different sound with their voices.

3. Go round again, this time adding a body sound to their first sound – they can make the two sounds together, or one after the other.

4. Go around a third time, adding a movement – at the same time as above, or consecutively.

5. Divide the class into small groups. Children organise their sounds and movement into a sequence or pattern which can be repeated.

6. Each group performs their sequence to the rest of the class and discusses success and problems:

   • How did you signal start and stop?
   • When did you stop thinking of ideas and start to practise?

EXTENSION

1. Create longer sequences of vocal sounds, body sounds and movements. This can be done sometimes by adding together several groups' or individuals' ideas one after the other.

2. Add changes to the sequences during the repetitions, for example, in pitch, dynamics, speed, tone.

PURPOSE
To develop children's skills in sequencing and group composition.

RESOURCES
A variety of sound sources.

REMEMBER

Always give quite short time limits for each stage working in groups – it concentrates the mind. Allow enough time for the refining and practising stages. Relate sounds and movements closely.

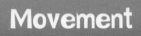

Two left feet

1. Practise the following rhyme until everyone knows it well:

>   >   >   >   >
>
> "He | had a good job and he | left, | left | left and it |
>
> >   >   >   >
>
> Jolly well served him | right | right | right." ‖

2. Spread out around the room. Practise marching – either on the spot or around in a circle – Left, right, left, right, etc.

3. As the children are marching, they say the rhyme out loud to themselves trying to say 'left' when the left foot is down and 'right' when the right foot is down:

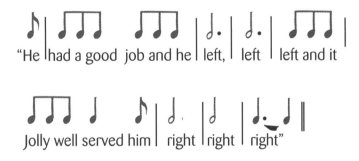

"He had a good job and he left, left left and it

Jolly well served him right right right"

4. It will take some individual practice for the children to be able to march and chant accurately without stopping the flow of the rhythm.

5. When it is mastered, try to work out, with the children, why it is so hard. There will be a tendency to skip at the end of the first line. The children are thereby recognising that an extra beat has been inserted into the rhythm of the rhyme.

EXTENSION

1. Encourage the children to talk about their own playground rhymes, hand games and passing games and look for the musical/rhythmic benefits in doing them together as a class.

PURPOSE

To enable children to understand what regular pulse is through carefully controlled movement.

REMEMBER

This is hard to do and you may find it hard to master yourself. Don't worry about trying it with the children and seeing if they can manage it before you. It gives them confidence if sometimes they are ahead of you.

A hint: You will need to wait before you say the second line to get it right.

Folk dancing

When taking children for folk dancing, remember that there are also considerable benefits for their musical development. Improved co-ordination helps in playing a musical instrument and exuberance in physical response to music encourages a love for it. This activity is to gain additional musical understanding through folk dancing, not to change the folk dancing activity itself. Think about the following things while you are dancing, in order to enhance that understanding.

1. Listen to some of the music first, asking children to notice certain aspects of it before you start dancing. For example: The rhythm, the mood, the repetitions of the tunes, the time.

2. Make sure that eventually no one counts out loud. Help the children to feel the phrases and internalise the pulse. For example. Circle to the right for 8, back again for 8.

3. Draw attention to the group movements that everyone does at the same time (circling, lines, in and out) and to the individual or couples' movements (in the centre of the circle, pairs down the line, hand movements).

4. A change of tune in folk music often indicates a change of mood or movement in the dance. Recognition of this contributes to good aural training. Help children to recognise when they are changing the dance at the point the melody changes.

EXTENSION

1. Traditional dance forms are usually just that, very traditional, and are not usually changed. However, children will benefit from working in small groups and coming up with some dance moves to reflect any type of music and musical phrases being played.

2. Children bring in music from their own home traditions to share with and teach others (maybe even their relatives to play the music on occasion).

PURPOSE

To help children to recognise specific musical skills that are enhanced through dancing, including musical phrases.
To refine physical control and response to music.

RESOURCES

Recordings, publications and instructions or downloads of folk dance music. Visit the Kickstart Music area of www.acblack.com/music for more resource ideas.

Drum with your feet

1. Check the children know their left and right.

   $\boxed{\text{LH}}$ = left hand $\boxed{\text{RH}}$ = right hand

   $\boxed{\text{LF}}$ = left foot $\boxed{\text{RF}}$ = right foot

2. Children sit at tables, with hands (LH/RH) on the table and feet (RF/LF) on the floor.

3. Everyone tries out the following combinations of actions (on the board or called out). Keep the pattern steady and continuous.

	1	2	3	4
a)	LF	LH	RH	RF :‖
b)	LH / LF	RH	LH / LF	RH :‖
c)	LH / LF	RH	RH	LH :‖
d)	RH / LF	LH LH	RH / LF	LH :‖

   and many more…

4. Children devise their own patterns and then try to maintain them.

EXTENSION

Children work in groups using their new drumming rhythm as the basis for accompanying a tune.

PURPOSE

To improve children's full body co-ordination and to recognise the skills needed to play a drum kit.

REMEMBER

Any pattern requires a lot of practice to perfect. When it becomes easy, make it more difficult by speeding it up.

Watch a film of a drummer at work to analyse their playing.

Tell a story

1. Listen to a short extract of the music with eyes closed.

2. Discuss with the children what they feel the mood of the music is, or what story it might be telling.

3. Play the music again and ask the children to experiment with movement to express their mood or story while it is being played.

4. Divide the children into groups of four or five. Give them time to agree both on a mood or story and a few movements to work with.

5. Play the music again for all the groups to try out their ideas. It may be necessary to repeat steps 4 and 5 more than once in order for the children to get their ideas clearly sorted out.

6. Share ideas with the rest of the class by performance and discussion.

PURPOSE
To develop children's expressive understanding through movement.

RESOURCES

Recordings of some strongly atmospheric music - eg. opening of Bartok's 'Music for Strings, Percussion and Celeste', or an early morning 'Rag'.

REMEMBER

Time for experimenting is essential.

Be careful not to direct the ideas too much. There are no right answers.

A ball in time

1. Children work in pairs, each pair with one ball. They spread out around the room.

2. Play the music. One child bounces and catches the ball in time to the music.

1	2	3		1	2	3
bounce	catch	wait		bounce	catch	wait

3. Change over. Play the music a second time. The other child in the pair tries to do the same and is watched by her partner.

4. Children move further apart. Play the music again. The children bounce the ball between them, still in time. They gradually move apart as they get better at it, bouncing the ball between them, still in time.

5. As they become more sure of the rhythm, the children exaggerate movements of bouncing and catching, or make the actions more graceful.

6. Change the style of throwing and the rhythm (eg, to 4 or 5 time).

EXTENSION

1. Use a drum, tambourine or the children's own music to move.

2. Children find other movements to include, eg, throw the ball on beat 1, clap on beat 2 and hop on the spot on beat 3.

PURPOSE

To develop the children's control and co-ordination in time to music.

RESOURCES

Enough balls for one between two children.

Music with a strong beat – preferably in 3 time.

Movement in sequence

1. Children find a space around the room. Listen to the music and swing arms in time to it.

2. Think of a new movement (eg clicking fingers, nodding heads, tapping feet), and change to it without missing a beat. Then change to another movement.

3. Everyone picks a bean bag. Think about how it is going to be used as part of the movement, eg waving it above your head, throwing it in the air.

4. Use the bag as part of the movement, passing it from one person to another.

5. Children divide into groups of 4 or 5. Ask the children to devise a sequence involving several different rhythmic movements and passing the bean bag from one to another.

6. Show sequences to the rest of the class.

EXTENSION

1. Use music with different pulses and speeds (eg waltz, blues, jig, march) to devise sequences of movements.

2. Use a ball or a rope, instead of a bean bag. These will require and produce a different range and rhythm of movements.

PURPOSE
To develop children's ability to co-ordinate movement in groups.

RESOURCES
Bean bags.

Recorded music with a strong, steady beat.

Journeys

PURPOSE
To develop a large movement and music performance project using all the children's previously learnt skills.

RESOURCES
The full range of instruments available, including keyboard, piano and computer software where possible. Some video footage of the chosen destination – eg, film of the Antarctic wastes and penguins.

REMEMBER
Give lots of short time-scales for each part of this project. Each section needs to be played and moved to with some success, before combining all the sections. Every part of the project can be treated as a separate activity.

1. Discuss with the class where they would like to go for a big adventure, for example: The moon, the Sahara, the Antarctic. We will use a journey to the Antarctic for the purposes of this activity.

2. Talk at some length about what they might find when they get there and how it would feel. Words such as empty, extreme, strange, freezing, and many more will be suggested.

3. Work on the movements they might need to use in a dance and music piece. Walking in snow shoes, swirling seas, penguins swimming and waddling, wrapping up warm, bracing against the wind, losing one's way, boats moving through water and ice to get there and get back.

4. Take one of these movements, (try bracing against the wind) and work on some music to go with it as a whole class. Remind the children of other musical pictures they have composed. It might include some of the following sounds:

   • Howling wind – vocal shushing, whistles, high screaming sounds on the recorder, high held notes on the keyboard, long flexible tubes swirling.

   • Stillness - wide open spaces: Quiet tap on cymbal, scattered hard notes on assorted chimes - silence.

   • Tents flapping in the wind – paper slapped on tables, notes played with several fingers at once on the keyboard or piano.

   • The feeling of leaning against the wind – slow, repetitive, low sounds on the piano with the pedal on or the bass guitar allowed to go on ringing, cymbal played with soft stick and left to ring.

   • Swirling seas – 'glissandi' up and down various pitched instruments, a slow rumbling sound on the low notes of various instruments, including clusters of electronic sounds.

5. One group of children practise this music while the others practise their movements. Put the music and the movements together and perform this section through.

6. In groups of no more than five, the children produce music for the other movement themes they have explored in point 3. Play each of these back to the class and discuss them and the ways they can improve their music.

7. Give more time to practise and improve their musical sections.

8. Each group plays their music while the rest of the children move to it. You may need to do this more than once to dovetail the two.

9. Initially, try putting two or three sections together consecutively to reflect the journey they are making to and from the Antarctic and the things that happen on the journey.

10. View, discuss with the class, and then choose some video footage that could be screened at the same time as the performance. Do not aim to integrate the film in with the music – use as a backcloth. Sea sounds might be heard and played alongside the music. Otherwise turn the sound off.

11. More time is needed to practise the layout of the final journey. It could be in simple formal structure – in the case below it is A, B, C, D, E, C, B, A. The various 'pictures' incorporated into the composition therefore might look like this:

A: On the boat on the high, swirling seas	B: Landing and watching the penguins
C: Walking about on the ice on snow shoes	D: Standing still listening to the silence
E: Bracing against the howling wind	C: More walking about in snow shoes
B: More penguins	A: Back on the boat returning home

12. Invite an audience such as another class, or parents at the end of the day, for the final performance. It would be ideal for an assembly or end of term performance.

This whole activity needs to be worked on over several sessions to develop children's confidence and skill sufficiently.

Slap, clap and click

1. With a group of about eight children, demonstrate the activity to the whole class.

2. Eight children sit in a circle. Number them 1 – 8.

3. Tap a regular rhythm and point to each child to say their number, one after the other, in order and in time, until they are confident.

4. With the children, set up a regular rhythm pattern with actions and practise it until it is secure. For example:

   Slap*, clap, click, click : repeat.
   *slap your thigh on the table.

5. Combine the two activities together. Person numbered 1 (maybe the teacher in the first instance) will say his number on the first click and then a different number on the second click:

   Slap, clap, click, click
            1   6

6. Child number 6 then says her number on the first click, followed by someone else's number on the second click:

   Slap, clap, click, click
            6   8

7. In effect, each numbered child is 'handing over' to the next numbered child. Continue until it breaks down. Start again with a new leader.

8. Divide the whole class into groups for each to play separately.

PURPOSE
To improve children's speed of response and their co-ordination skills.

REMEMBER

Keep the pulse very steady, perhaps in the first instance with a regular beat on a triangle, quiet enough to be there but barely heard.

This section includes activities which will help children to find their voice, sing with enjoyment and musicality, improve their pitch discrimination and begin to improvise music. Some will also help children to understand the role of simple notations to record music.

Pitch perfect

Try any or all of these activities for about five minutes at the beginning of any session using the voice. Stand up evenly on both feet to make sure the body is as relaxed as possible.

1. **Breathing and breath control.**
   a) Breathe in for 2 counts – blow out gently for 4 counts – later for 8 counts.
   b) Breathe in for 2 counts – hum for 4 counts and then later, 6, 8 up to 12 counts.
   c) Pull tummy muscles in quickly; this will make air escape from the mouth (it should sound like a 'h'). Do not blow to make the sound. Repeat 4 or 8 times, (this will be exercising and strengthening your diaphragm).

2. **Consonants for articulation.**

   a) | Teacher | Class all together |
      |---------|--------------------|
      | P | p |
      | Ch | ch |
      | T | t |
      | Ggggg | ggggg |
      | Ccccc | ccccc |

   b) Sing up and down a few notes with different consonants repeated, see right.

      Do it faster and faster or do it very slowly making each consonant explosive and the sound which follows as warm as possible.

Ssssss
Mmmmm
Ccccccc
Pppppp

3. **Pitch practice.**
   Sing up the scale to a variety of silly sounds using all the vowels such as: ning, nang, noo; bing, bang bong; fee, fie, foe, fum.

PURPOSE
To ensure the voice is properly warmed up before using it to sing or as a sound source.

One by one

1. Introduce the tune to the class. Sing it line by line and the children repeat each line to remind themselves of how it goes.

2. Sing the whole song with the children joining in until they can sing it all the way through securely.

3. Divide the class into two groups. Alternate the phrases of the song. The two groups sing alternating phrases, for example:

   Group 1 'God save our gracious Queen
   Group 2   Long live our noble Queen' etc

4. Next sing the song word by word or note by note:

   Group 1   'God'   Group 2   'Save'
                 'our'   'gra-'
                 '-cious'   'Queen' and so on.

   Can the class keep in tune and in time all the way through?

5. Divide the class into smaller groups, or try it with one child singing at a time round the circle.

EXTENSION

Try sending the tune to the right and to the left simultaneously round the circle.

PURPOSE
To improve children's accuracy of pitch in singing.

RESOURCES

Songs that are familiar to the whole class. Here the example of 'God save the Queen' is used.

REMEMBER

Encourage correct pitch and rhythm. If there are gaps while you wait for someone to sing his bit, it does not sound like the tune any more.

Shape the sound

PURPOSE
To encourage children to use instruments and voices imaginatively.

RESOURCES

A long line drawn on the board or paper.

1. Discuss with the class the wiggly line drawn on the board. Talk about it in musical terms of low, high, ups and downs, loud and soft.

2. Find ways to represent the line in sound:
    a) With voices.
    b) With instruments.
    c) With different pitch or volume.

3. A few individual children try to represent the line on an instrument. Listen to, and discuss, their ideas.

4. Children move into groups. and try ways to 'play' it.

5. Share all ideas within the class by each group 'performing' and discussing. Play several, one after another, to make a longer piece.

EXTENSION

1. Children draw their own lines and try to reproduce them in the same way.

2. Try using two lines at once – one for voices and one for instruments, eg.

3. Listen to a song or solo instrument (maybe performed by one of the children) and try drawing the line of the melody. Comment on any repetitive patterns you find.

See and Play

1. Display all the flash cards (see below). Choose one of them and play or sing it to the children. Any notes will do provided that they represent the high, middle or low position of the dots.

2. Children work out which card is being played or sung.

3. Turn all cards upside down and ask each child to pick one at random. The children play the cards on an instrument or chime bars of their own choice.

PURPOSE

To develop children's understanding of the way in which tunes develop and are written down.

RESOURCES

A variety of chime bars or other pitched instruments.

A set of flash cards with simple patterns.

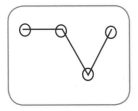
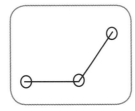
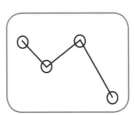
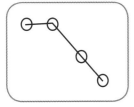
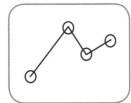
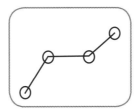

EXTENSION

1. Arrange the cards one after another to create a musical pattern. Play the pattern through and discuss the music created, for example, Does that sound good played twice? Should we switch anything around?

2. Make any changes to the order of the cards and play the new pattern through, discussing the effect on the music and any more changes needed to improve it.

3. Try to notate the tunes that result:

   Play from this copy.

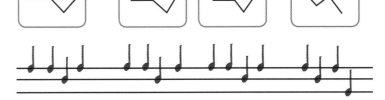

4. Children design their own flash cards and play or sing them.

Treasure Hunt

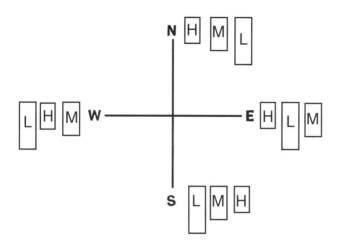

PURPOSE

To encourage children to listen for variations in pitch.

RESOURCES

A large treasure map on paper or board with grid lines north/south and east/west marked on it to produce squares. (This could be made in a previous art seession with the class).

Counters and chime bars.

1. Arrange the chime bars into four sets of three notes – a high (H), medium (M) and low (L) note in each group. Make sure the children can understand the principle.

2. Allocate each set to a point of the compass (see illustration). Check the children can recognise the sound of each set and which direction they will move in.

3. Set out the treasure map plus the counters in the middle of the room with the children sitting around it. Play one of the sets of notes, repeating if necessary. Children listen and decide which direction it represents.

4. One child picks a counter and moves their counter in to the position that the music has directed them, for example:
   – Teacher plays H M L - player moves one square to the north.
   – Teacher plays L H M - player moves one square to the west.

5. This activity can be played in pairs, groups or as a class.

EXTENSION
1. Children can produce their own map and make up their own code for directions.

2. Make simpler instructions: Maracas mean up two, drum means down four etc.

3. Make the game harder by using specific pitches eg. B = up, A = down.

Match the note

1. Set the chime bars in alphabetical order in a circle. Choose one child to sit by each chime bar.

2. Another child sits behind each of the chime bar children. Set out the tuned instruments (eg, xylophone or glockenspiel) amongst the second ring of children so that all of the children in this ring have access to an instrument.

3. Choose a child from the second ring and ask them to play a note from their instrument. Ask the child with the corresponding chime bar to play it.

4. The class discusses by raising or lowering thumbs whether the chime bar player has been accurate. The tuned percussion instrument player repeats their note until the correct chime bar is played.

5. Repeat the procedure with a different note.

6. Change around the players in the chime bar line and the children playing the tuned percussion instruments around to give everyone a turn.

7. Ask a child to play a chime bar. Children find the sound on their tuned percussion.

This activity is slightly harder if the two notes are concords (3rds, 4ths, 5ths, octaves), and easier if they are discords (2nds and 7ths). Make sure that they hear examples of both concord and discord intervals on their chosen instruments.

PURPOSE
To encourage increasing accuracy in differentiating between levels of pitch.

RESOURCES

Seven chime bars in alphabetical order.

Glockenspiel, xylophone or metallophone with notes to match the chime bars. Or the piano could be used if an even greater discrimination and facility is expected.

REMEMBER

This activity can be continued during 'free' time between sessions, if tuned percussion is made available as a 'music area' activity. Don't forget – this counts towards music curriculum time.

Two chord tunes

1. Make sure the notes of your instrument are arranged in order:
   C, D, E, F, G, A , B, C, D, E,

2. Find the C chord. The three notes of a chord are always: 1st note – leave a gap – 3rd note – leave a gap - 5th note. The ☐C chord is therefore C E G –see below

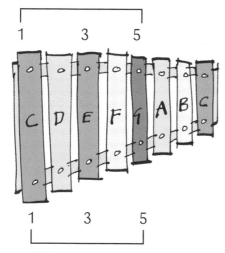

3. Find a ☐G chord in the same way: 1st note G – leave a gap – 3rd note B – leave a gap – fifth note D.

4. Demonstrate to the class how to play the two chords using six children to model it.

5. Three children play the ☐C chord together, C,E,G.

6. Three more children play the ☐G chord together, G,B,D.

7. Practise changing from one chord to the other and keeping 'good time'. If you have enough instruments, put children into 'chord' groups (a group for ☐G , another for ☐C). They play the two chords changing them as below.

   ☐C 2 3 4 ☐G 2 3 4 ☐G 2 3 4 ☐C 2 3 4

EXTENSION

Try playing the chords along with a well known tune eg 'Hush little baby' (see right) or 'Oh my darling Clementine'. The melody lines for these tunes can be found at the Kickstart Music area of www.acblack.com/music.

PURPOSE
To extend children's understanding of harmony by using two chords.

RESOURCES
Chime bars or other pitched instruments. For this activity, avoid bars that have a sharp symbol (#) or a flat symbol (b).

Hush little baby

Don't say a word

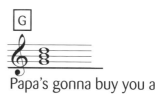
Papa's gonna buy you a

Mocking bird

Motifs

1. Divide the children into groups of four.

2. Ask them to chant their first names rhythmically and decide in which order they should be performed.

eg. John   Marjorie   Leroy   Vikesh

3. Make sure they are secure by asking the children to clap their sequences.

4. Give each group pitched instruments and ask them to work out a tune for their sequences using notes from a pentatonic scale, for example:

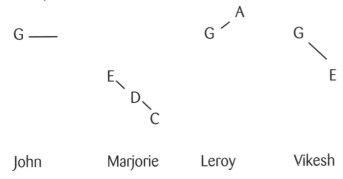

John   Marjorie   Leroy   Vikesh

5. Bring the groups together and listen to their tunes. Discuss an order for all of the tunes to make a class composition. Decide which group's tune would start it well and which would finish it. Try various combinations.

6. Try playing two sections of the class composition at the same time.

EXTENSION

1. Use other word rhythms, eg, favourite food, names of vegetables.

2. Sing the tunes of the names around the class.

PURPOSE
To invent a tune using a pentatonic scale, using the children's names as a rhythmic framework.

RESOURCES

Chime bars, glockenspiels, xylophones.

Keyboard or piano – black notes only.

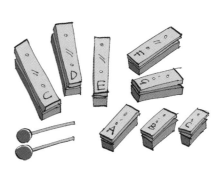

Singing intervals

1. Make sure the notes of the instruments are arranged in order C, D, E, F, G, A, B, C.

2. Be sure that the concept of intervals is understood by looking at Intervals and Moods (page 59).

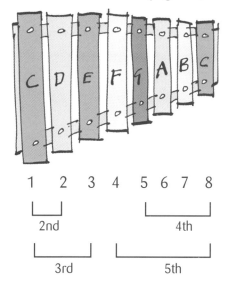

3. Play the intervals to the class and ask the children to sing them in answer. Remember the numbers are inclusive:

> C – E = 3rd
> C – F = 4th
> C – G = 5th

4. Ask the children to identify the intervals by ear - they will have to sing or 'think' the notes in the gaps before they can answer. Intervals can start on any note, for example, F – C is a fifth (see above).

5. Ask a child to sing an interval above a note sounded, eg, play or sing F and ask child to sing a 3rd above. Play A to check they have it right.

EXTENSION

Children work in pairs. One sings a note, names it and says an interval. The second child plays (or sings) their note at the required interval.

PURPOSE

To develop children's accuracy in both singing and hearing intervals.

RESOURCES

Xylophones, glockenspiels, chime bars, keyboards.

REMEMBER

This is not just one lesson – it is a long process to train the ear. Three minutes every day for weeks would help.

Accompanying songs

with harmony

PURPOSE

To expand the number of ways children can accompany songs with some harmony.

RESOURCES

A song book with guitar chord letters above – there are a number of examples on the website, www. acblack.com/music. Visit the Kickstart Music area.

Xylophone, glockenspiel, keyboard or chime bars.

1. Decide on a song with guitar chord letters above it.
    Sing it confidently with the class.

2. Play each chord letter with each marked word as in the activity 'Two chord tunes' p47. Start the song on note A.

    eg. Dm

    What shall we do with a drunken sailor?

    C

    What shall we do with a drunken sailor?

    Dm

    What shall we do with a drunken sailor?

    C   Dm

    Early in the morning.

3. Make it more interesting by giving the chord note or chord letter a rhythm which plays the speech of part of the song and use it as an introduction.
    For example:

    Dm   Dm

    (What shall we do with the) What shall we do with the drunken sailor?

EXTENSION

1. If chords have been well enough understood, try giving the children the job of finding the full chords:

    Dm = D F A   C = C E G   F = F A C   G = G B D

2. Use an electronic keyboard to accompany the songs. There are settings on most keyboards which allow you to play just the bass note and the full chord will play. However, make sure that, when children use those settings, they have first understood how the chord is constructed by doing activities such as the above.

3. There are many other songs which have a limited range of chords which can be used to accompany them. Here's another one.

    C   C

    Red and yellow and pink and green,

    F   C   G

    Purple and orange and blue.

    C   F

    I can sing a rainbow,

    C   C

    Sing a rainbow,

    C   G   C

    Sing a rainbow too.

Accompanying songs

With drones and ostinati

PURPOSE
To enable children
to extend ways of
accompanying a song.

1. Choose a song which is based on a pentatonic scale. For
   example:

Li'l Liza Jane	C, D, E, G, A	(start on note E)
Old MacDonald	D, E, G, A, B	(start on note G)
Skye Boat Song	D, E, G, A, B	(start on note D)

2. Sing the song several times with the class to make sure
   everyone is singing confidently.

3. Divide the children into groups. They take any two notes from
   the chosen scale (see the notes of the scales above) and play
   them regularly and rhythmically while the song is being sung –
   like the 'drone' on the bagpipes.
   For example:

(Intro.................)   Speed - bonny   boat - like a

RESOURCES

Pitched instruments
and voices.

Well known songs.

There is a glossary
of musical terms, eg,
drones and ostinati
at the Kickstart Music
section of www.
acblack.com/music.

EXTENSION

1. Ask the children to find an ostinato instead of (or as well as) a
   drone, ie. a repeated pattern of notes throughout the song.

G
E
(Intro.......................)   Old   Mac-Donald   had   a   farm...

Make sure 'pentatonic' is understood through using the activity
'Motifs' on p48.

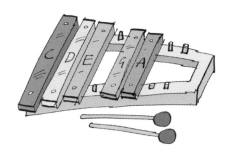

Sounds and Invention

This section includes activities which will encourage children to discover and develop their own library of musical sounds, ways to combine those sounds to make musical patterns and sequences, and ways to improvise musical ideas. They will be given opportunities to invent their own music, refine it and perform it to others.

Haiku

1. Introduce the poems, reading them expressively. Discuss the language used and the overall feel of each poem.

2. Talk about the idea of 'word painting' and how one particular word or phrase could be expressed in music.

3. Divide the children into groups and give each group a poem. Ask them to nominate a narrator to make the words of the poem an integral part of the music.

4. Give the children time to compose their own piece that expresses the atmosphere of their poem.

5. Perform the pieces and encourage discussion by other children of each performance. They can either choose to work with the words, or make the music express the feeling of the words on its own.

6. Children make up their own haiku and compose music to suit it. Perform it to the class or to an invited audience.

PURPOSE

To explore the composition of atmospheric/ expressive music, using poetry as a stimulus.

RESOURCES

Haiku poems (Japanese poems based on the syllable pattern 5–7-5 - see examples).

A variety of classroom instruments or sound sources.

Haiku

Mountain – Rose Petals
Falling falling, falling now
Waterfall music.
             'Basho'

Mirror - pond of stars
Suddenly a summer shower
Dimples the water.
                      'Sora'

Seas are wild tonight ...
Stretching over Sado island
Silent clouds of stars.
             'Basho'

Silent the old town
The scent of flowers, floating
And evening bell.
                      Bisho'

Making patterns

Do one or more of the following at the beginning of a music session:

1. **Body sounds.** Teacher starts and children copy.

   Hands:
   Shake them as hard as possible and listen. Rub them on your sleeve and legs and listen. Wiggle your fingers and rub them against each other and listen. Do it rhythmically, for example:
   Clap, clap, wave, wave, clap, clap, wave, wave...
   Click, click, thighs, thighs, click, click, thighs, thighs...
   Rub head, rub head, tap head, tap head...

   Feet:
   Shuffle, shuffle, slide, slide, shuffle, shuffle, slide, slide...
   Stamp, stamp, hop, hop, stamp, stamp, hop, hop...

   Repeat the patterns and then add new ones and repeat. Listen all the time to the sounds they make. Children take turns to lead or work in pairs to find new sounds.

2. **Sound makers.** Use the tables, radiators, walls, chairs in the room to explore a new range of sounds and patterns. Use a stick or pencil – scrape, rub, tap, hit. Find sounds from junk materials, for example:

   - Plastic bottles – fill with different materials (pulses, clips, sugar). Screw cap on tightly.
   - Blowing bubbles in a drink carton – through a straw and humming.
   - Brushes for sweeping sounds and rhythms.
   - Paper – use assorted paper to tug, rip, scrunch, flap, brush, flick, blow.

   Try making sounds and patterns with: A rubber band; a pencil case; a glove; a storage box; a pen; a cup; anything else around; two of them together.

3. Children make patterns of two different sound patterns in pairs. Play them to the class and keep repeating the patterns until the rhythm is very secure. You could use the rhythm that emerges to accompany someone singing a simple song.

PURPOSE
To reinforce the use of body sounds and various simple sound makers in musical pattern making.

RESOURCES
Tables, chairs and other objects around the room.
Junk materials.

REMEMBER
Pattern making in music is very important indeed. Find a sound or sequence of sounds of any kind, keep repeating it till it makes a regular rhythmic pattern. Add another rhythmic pattern. Repeat the first one and so on. Use patterns to accompany singing or dancing.

The sea

1. Discuss with the class which sounds might be heard at the seaside and out at sea.

2. Make a list of everyone's ideas, for example:
   – waves breaking on rocks, sea gulls, ship sirens, wind, sails, storm waves. View video if available.

3. Children divide into groups. Each group chooses a sea sound from the list. They experiment with voices, instruments and/ or other sound sources, including the keyboard, computer software or the Internet, to find appropriate sounds or sequences to go with it.

4. Each group demonstrates their sound sequence to the rest of the class. Discuss how effective it is. See if the class can guess which sea sounds they used.

5. Create a longer piece by linking all of the groups' musical sequences together. Direct each group when to play and when to stop.

6. Spend time discussing what order the sounds work best in, and if any need repeating. Give time for practice.

7. Play again with any modifications made, to make a musical seascape. Choose a conductor from the class to do the same for a repeat performance.

EXTENSION

1. Record the musical seascape – listen and modify the performance accordingly.

2. Find some sea music audio and video material on the web and discuss it.

3. Make a graphic or pictorial score of the piece. Listen to sea music others have written (see resource box).

PURPOSE
To enable children to invent a piece of sea music.

RESOURCES

A variety of instruments, including, if possible, keyboard and/or computer software. Voices. Video of the sea (optional - from the Internet).

Sea music for example,

• 'Four Sea interludes' from 'Peter Grimes' by Benjamin Britten.

• 'Hebrides Overture', by Mendelssohn .

• 'La Mer,' Debussy.

Opposite moods

1. With the class, make a list of contrasting emotions or moods, For example:

> Love – hate
> Sad – happy
> Frightened– brave
> Excited – calm

2. Discuss the character of each mood in terms of colours, facial expression, movements, tone of voice, pitch, dynamics, speed. Can the children come up with any more characteristics?

3. Children work in groups of 4 or 5 and invent a sequence of sounds which describes a mood, using a variety of instrumental sounds or voices.

> eg. group 1 – happy   group 3 – frightened
>   group 2 – sad   group 4 – brave

4. Allow plenty of time to experiment and invent. Encourage the children to use words as well if they wish.

5. Each group performs their mood piece for the class.

EXTENSION

1. Create a longer piece of different moods. Each group plays one after another, matching opposite moods together, making a musical structure of contrasts.

Happy (grp 1)	Sad (grp 2)	Happy (grp 1)
Frightened (grp 3)	Brave (grp 4)	Frightened (grp 3)

2. Use role play to provide a context for exploring varying moods eg, calming an angry child, receiving a birthday present.

3 Explore ways to write the music down using colours and symbols.

4. Record the results. Listen and discuss.

PURPOSE
To enable children to explore and create music which communicates a variety of emotions.

RESOURCES

A variety of instruments.

Voices.

Musical plans

1. Introduce a plan to the children (see below). Discuss the different parts together. Explain and discuss the language involved, eg, long, short, high and low. You might want to use the Italian words for short and long, for example, 'staccato' and 'legato'. See a full musical glossary online at the Kickstart Music area of www.acblack.com/music.

2. Practise and perform the plan together as a class using voices.

3. Split the children into groups. Give them their own plan and ask them to practise and perform with a variety of instruments.

4. Discuss the performances, focussing on how each part of the performance links to the plan that they were given.

5. If possible record the performances so that the children can listen to their own work and evaluate it.

PURPOSE

To encourage children to explore the different characteristics of sound and to further develop technical language and the use of graphic scores.

RESOURCES

Variety of classroom instruments or sounds.

Variety of large musical plans.

Glossary online at www.acblack.com/music.

START					
S I L E N C E	Lots of short/high sounds	One loud/long sound	Six soft sounds played slowly	3 loud short sounds	
	Sequence of 2 long and 1 short sound	1 2 ___ 3 ___ 1 2 ___ 3 ___ 1 2 ___ 3 ___			
	Lots of short/high sounds	One loud/long sound	Six soft sounds played slowly	3 loud short sounds	S I L E N C E
					STOP

The science of sound

1. Investigate pitch:

Lay the tubes over the resonating board (eg, an open box that allows objects to ring).

- Which has the highest/lowest/loudest sound?
- Arrange them in order – lowest to highest.
- Is the longest/fattest the lowest and why?
- What are the tubes made of? Does it matter?

2. Investigate amplification:

- Stretch out a large band between two children and pluck it. Can it be heard at the back?
- Stretch it over an open box. What is the difference?
- Play a xylophone note both on and off the instrument and compare the difference of the sounds.
- List the instruments that have 'sound boxes' – violin, guitar, bass, piano. What about the voice?
- Try a funnel – blow a raspberry down a tube both without, and then with, the funnel on the end.
- Place a piece of thin card between the bar and the hole of a chime bar. Tap the chime bar and slide the card back and forth over the hole. What happens?

3. Investigate vibration:

- Which tubes ring the longest/shortest/not at all? Why?
- What are the tubes made of?
- Discuss the terms 'resonance' and 'vibrations'.
- Find objects that visibly vibrate and make a sound:
- Use the rubber band guitar on the box.
- Play a plastic ruler on the edge of a table.
- Hit a cymbal. When does it stop vibrating?
- Place cling film tightly over a box for a drum.
- Tap a triangle then whilst it is still vibrating (sounding) lower into a bowl of water.

4. Make music with any of the above.

PURPOSE

To enable children to explore and understand how sound is made.

RESOURCES

Resonating board (eg, and open box that allows objects to ring), tubes of different length and width, rubber bands, funnel, boxes, cymbal and various other materials, eg. paper, copper, plastic etc.

More information can be found in the Kickstart Music area of www.acblack.com/music.

Intervals and Moods

1. Make sure the notes of the instruments are arranged in alphabetical order C, D, E, F, G, A, B, C. Look at it vertically like a ladder.

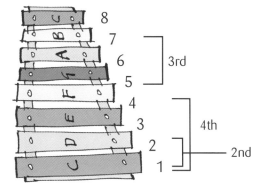

'Intervals' are the gaps between notes
C to D = 1 – 2 = a second
D to C = 2 – 8 = a seventh
E to A = 3 – 6 = a fourth

2. Remember to count inclusively – E, F, G, A/1, 2, 3, 4 = 4th. Make sure the class understands this thoroughly before proceeding.

3. Choose an interval of a 2nd, eg: B–C or E–F. A child plays both notes together repeatedly very slowly - like a heart beat. What does it make the class think of/feel? They might say for this interval: Strange, frightening, waiting.

4. Choose an interval of a 4th, eg, C– F. A child uses hard sticks and plays both notes together rhythmically and strongly. What does it make the class think of/feel? They might say: Warlike, proud, procession.

5. Try 3rds – eg, C–E or D–F. Some thirds may sound quite cheerful (major). Some may sound quite sombre or sad (minor intervals). Some children may be able to work out which is which and why.

6. Children work in groups making a piece using one of the intervals/moods – 2nds, 3rds or 4ths. Record the result when children are satisfied.

PURPOSE
To give children simple devices for exploring different moods through music.

RESOURCES

Xylophones, glockenspiels, chime bars.

Try 'Singing intervals' p49 first.

REMEMBER

Each interval gives a different feeling which can be used for particular effects in future. Each child will describe the feeling in different ways. There are no absolutely right answers here. The suggestions above are only given for guidance.

Forms and patterns

1. Working in pairs, children invent very short tunes, rhythms or musical ideas and the whole class listens to them in turn.

2. Choose three of these tunes to begin with for a class piece. Label them tunes A, B and C.

3. Listen to all three with the class and decide in which order to play the tunes. They might decide A, C, B, C, A.

4. Children to play the tunes in order and decide if the choice was a good one by asking questions like:
   - Is it long/too short?
   - How could we make it longer?
   - Did we start and stop well?
   - Do we need an introduction or a clearer ending?
   - Do the tunes fit together well?
   - Would it be better to change the order/repeat?
   - What does it sound like to play two tunes concurrently?
   - Would one tune be better on another instrument?

5. Make final decisions as a class. Practise and perform the final piece.

6. Record the piece. Give it a name which will help you all to remember it. Some children might like to try and write its structure down to save for the future.

EXTENSION

Children work in smaller groups making pieces by themselves, inventing more than one idea.

PURPOSE

To extend children's understanding of how music is put together and structured, in patterns of musical ideas.

RESOURCES

A variety of instruments, at least one per group, with at least one pitched instrument per group.

REMEMBER

Composing music is about choosing what sounds and musical ideas to use, when and how often. Lots of listening, discussion and practice time is needed.

Exploring keyboards

Investigating the piano

1. Lift up the piano lid and remove the front to show the inner workings.

2. Disover with all the children, or in groups at different times, what a piano can do and how it does it:
   - How a sound is made?
   - What causes notes to be loud or soft?
   - What makes notes long or short?
   - What do pedals do?
   - Why do strings vary in length and thickness?
   - What's the difference in sounds between a piano hammer hitting the string and a beater gently hitting a string?

3. Write up the investigation and look up the history of the piano in books/on the Web.

Investigating the electronic keyboard

1. Display the keyboard clearly, perhaps propped up at an angle. Select a button, eg, a violin sound. Hold one note down and list descriptions of the sound.

2. Discover more about the keyboard:
   - What are the different sounds available?
   - What rhythm functions are there?
   - How can we play along with the rhythm functions?
   - Find ways of making the rhythms fast or slow.

3. Give the children time to explore and use other functions on the keyboard, eg, the automatic chords and the full range of instrumental buttons.

4. Try to play some of the rhythms from the keyboard on percussion instruments. Children will have to listen very carefully to do this.

5. Write up their investigation and look up the short history of the electronic keyboard on the Web.

PURPOSE
To investigate and explore different types of sound sources.

RESOURCES
Piano, electric keyboard, paper, pencils, beaters.

REMEMBER
An electric keyboard and piano can be used as a sound source for any of the activities in this book requiring pitched instruments for two or three children to use together. Go back to many of the invention activities in this book and use the keyboard and/or the piano as an additional or central instrument for the composition.

School Exhibition

PURPOSE

To give children more experience of composition using their own art work as a stimulus, and bringing together elements of all the children's musical experience.

RESOURCES

Some of the children's own art work.

A recording of 'Pictures at an Exhibition' by Mussorgsky.

A variety of instruments, including keyboard and computer-generated sound sources.

Before you begin the activity, play the children extracts from a recording of 'Pictures at an Exhibition' by Mussorgsky.

1. Explain how Mussorgsky's piece illustrates a walk through an art exhibition and how it is constructed:

   Promenade – Picture A, Promenade – Picture B, Promenade – Picture C

   Listen to three sections – for example, the Promenade and two of the pictures, to get an idea of what the project entails.

2. Divide the children into groups of a maximum of five children. Each group chooses a painting/drawing from their own art work to represent with a piece of music.

3. Choose one group to compose a 'walking piece' that will link all of the musical pictures together.

4. Ask each group to discuss and choose instruments or sound sources needed. They explore the possibilities of those resources first. Then they work on a composition of a 30 second piece to illustrate their picture. Encourage the use of some of the following:
   - Interesting repeated patterns.
   - Sequences of notes and phrases.
   - Repetition of both the above.
   - Layering of sounds, more than one idea going on at the same time.
   - Contrasts – loud/soft, fast/slow, dark/light, staccato/legato.

5. Listen to each group's piece several times as it is worked on. Give plenty of time to develop it and practise it to make a polished performance.

6. Put it all together as a class piece. Decide on the order of the paintings to be 'looked at' between the walking round music. For example it might be in this order:

   Walk – **A** – Walk – **B** – Walk – **C** - Walk – **D**– Walk

7. When ready, perform the whole piece together. Discuss and evaluate the performance and composition.

8. Give them more time to perfect their pieces and play again. Record the result.

EXTENSION

1. Place large posters from different places around the classroom wall, eg. a sea scene, a volcano erupting, a busy street scene.

2. Devise a musical walk around the classroom listening to everyone's musical pictures of the posters.

3. Bring in another class to listen.

4. Work on this alongside a visit to a local exhibition – or use a selection of art images from the Web.

5. It could work well as a full day's activity for an 'Activities Week' at the end of term. Alternatively each picture could be done by each class in the school for an end of term performance to parents.

REMEMBER

If the performance works well, let a long silence remain at the end. Don't feel the need to talk about it. Let the sound stay in the children's mind for as long as possible.

This activity will work best if done over several music sessions, or in groups in a 'music area', bringing it all together at the end.

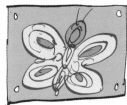

Resources

EQUIPMENT

Many of the activities in the book can be done without any instruments or soundmakers, or with simple sound makers (such as home-made or found objects), but it is always desirable to build a collection of good quality and easily accessible instruments. **Pitched instruments** might include xylophones, glockenspiels, chime bars and ocarinas, as well as piano, keyboards and other instruments children are learning in school, such as steel pans, trumpets or violins. **Unpitched percussion instruments** might include various sized drums and tablas, cymbals, bells and other resonant instruments, tambourines, rattles and other shakers, guiros and other scrapers. **Good quality beaters** are very important in getting the best quality sound from these instruments.

SONGS AND ACTIVITIES

No list could ever be comprehensive in an area such as this. There are many more songbooks as well than those listed here and teachers will have a list of their own songs whilst being unaware of the origins. Some examples include 'Okki-Tokki-Unga', 'Three Singing Pigs', 'Three Rapping Pigs', 'Banana Splits', 'Sonsense Nongs', 'Bobby Shaftoe, Clap your Hands', 'Someone's Singing, Lord' and 'Tam Tam Tambalay'. For details and a full song index visit www.acblack.com/music

RECORDED MUSIC

Recent major advances in technology mean that every classroom with a computer and amplification (eg, via a whiteboard system) can now play (and record) music. With the ease of use of the internet CD's are looking dated. Compilation CDs offer a useful introduction to listening, and music educational shops and publications often provide music suitable for use in early years and primary schools. Substantial information and guidance is to be found at the Kickstart Music area of the website (www.acblack.com/music).

Use the internet to access:

- Music for listening, either online, to stream or as downloads.
- Video clips for composition, to watch or to download.
- Free software for composing and manipulating music.

This list is in no way exhaustive or prescriptive and there are more ideas on the website. It is merely a list of music used successfully by many teachers for activities like these. There has been no attempt to include suggestions for modern popular music in this list, not as a result of any value judgement, but because fashion and availability is continually changing:

- **Albinoni** Adagio
- **Benjamin** Jamaican Rumba
- **Berlioz** Symphonie Fantastique
- **Brubeck** Unsquare Dance
- **Debussy** La Mer
- **Dukas** The Sorcerer's Apprentice
- **Glass (Philip)** Glassworks
- **Holst** The Planets Suite
- **McCartney** Yesterday and other songs
- **Mendelssohn** The Hebrides Overture
- **Prokofiev** Peter and the Wolf
- **Saint-Saëns** Carnival of the Animals
- **Vaughan Williams** Fantasia on Greensleeves
- **Stravinsky** Petrushka
- **Vivaldi** Four Seasons

FOR MORE INFORMATION ON RESOURCES AND A FULL SONG LIST VISIT WWW.ACBLACK.COM/MUSIC